Martin Taylor's

JAZZ**GUITAR**LICKS PHRASE**BOOK**

Over 100 Beginner & Intermediate Licks for Jazz Guitar

MARTIN**TAYLOR**
WITH JOSEPH**ALEXANDER**

FUNDAMENTAL**CHANGES**

Martin Taylor's Jazz Guitar Licks Phrase Book

Over 100 Beginner & Intermediate Licks for Jazz Guitar

ISBN: 978-1-78933-212-4

Published by **www.fundamental-changes.com**

www.fundamental-changes.com

Over 11,000 fans on Facebook: **FundamentalChangesInGuitar**

Instagram: **FundamentalChanges**

For over 350 Free Guitar Lessons with Videos Check Out

www.fundamental-changes.com

Cover Image Copyright: Lister Cumming, used with permission.

Contents

About the Authors

Dr Martin Taylor MBE is a virtuoso guitarist, composer, educator and musical innovator.

Acoustic Guitar magazine has called him, "THE acoustic guitarist of his generation." Chet Atkins said that Martin is, "One of the greatest and most impressive guitarists in the world," and Pat Metheny commented that, "Martin Taylor is one of the most awesome solo guitar players in the history of the instrument."

Widely considered to be the world's foremost exponent of solo jazz and fingerstyle guitar playing, Martin possesses an inimitable style that has earned him global acclaim from fellow musicians, fans and critics alike. He dazzles audiences with a signature style which artfully combines his virtuosity, emotion and humour with a strong, engaging stage presence.

Martin has enjoyed a remarkable musical career spanning five decades, with more than 100 recordings to his credit. Completely self-taught, beginning at the early age of 4, he has pioneered a unique way of approaching solo jazz guitar that he now breaks down into seven distinct stages in order to teach others.

Joseph Alexander is one of the most prolific writers of modern guitar tuition methods.

He has sold over 600,000 books that have educated and inspired a generation of upcoming musicians. His uncomplicated tuition style is based around breaking down the barriers between theory and performance, and making music accessible to all.

Educated at London's Guitar Institute and Leeds College of Music, where he earned a degree in Jazz Studies, Joseph has taught thousands of students and written over 40 books on playing the guitar.

He is the managing director of *Fundamental Changes Ltd.*, a publishing company whose sole purpose is to create the highest quality music tuition books and pay excellent royalties to writers and musicians.

Fundamental Changes has published over 120 music tuition books and is currently accepting submissions from prospective authors and teachers of all instruments. Get in touch via **webcontact@fundamental-changes.com** if you'd like to work with us on a project.

Introduction from Martin

Hi there, and welcome to my beginner jazz guitar licks phrase book.

I want to begin by asking you a question. If you were to visit another country and needed to communicate in another language, would it be more useful to be given a dictionary or a phrase book?

Of course, that's an easy answer. If you don't even know the words you need, how on earth would you find them in a dictionary? However, given a phrase book, you can immediately copy the sounds and begin to communicate. As you gradually learn more phrases from your book and copy the sounds that people are making, you'll start to combine them and suddenly you're beginning to speak.

The quickest way to learn to communicate in a new language is always to learn some phrases and copy the sounds that native speakers make. You won't reach for the dictionary or use a "theory of language" grammar book, you'll just directly copy some language you've heard and apply it in a real-life situation.

This is why it continues to astonish me that people treat learning the language of jazz guitar any differently. I've had students approach me who know far more theory than me – all the clever scales and arpeggios they *could* use on this or that chord – but when they actually play the guitar, more often than not their solos just don't sound jazzy. Guitarists are often guilty of taking a "theory first" approach to learning jazz because they've been told that jazz is "hard" or "all about the theory". The reality is, playing jazz is much simpler than you might think. Often, the great players we idolise are playing fairly simple ideas, just with great time and phrasing.

How did they develop this phrasing? By copying and playing the language of the musicians *they* admired.

This book is all about learning the language of jazz guitar, and you're going to do this by listening to me play some of my favourite phrases. Having learnt them, you'll incorporate them into your own playing. You'll copy my notes, phrasing and rhythms. You'll learn hundreds of pieces of *vocabulary*. You'll begin to combine these into sentences that will grow to form solos. As you do this, you'll begin to understand how the language of jazz soloing sounds and *feels*.

You may be thinking, "But what about the *theory!*" My answer to that is that you didn't learn to speak with a book of grammar in your hand, you copied the adults around you. Maybe some theory came a little later when you were at school and you learnt about adjectives and verbs and iambic pentameter, but I'm sure you were doing a wonderful job of speaking before you were introduced to these complex ideas.

In this book, there is no theory! There's just language, phrases and the vocabulary that forms the basis of the rich jazz language. I made a conscious decision *not* to include lick breakdowns because I want you to focus solely on the communication and *voice* of your music.

These phrases are organised so that you can use them over very common chord progressions in jazz. The popular chord sequences that occur in most jazz standards are here. Don't worry if you spot a sequence I've not covered – this book isn't supposed to be an exhaustive list of licks you can play in every possible situation. Once you've learned to speak, you will quickly be able to apply the phrasing and language to any chord sequence you like.

Have fun!

Martin Taylor

April 2020

A Note from Joseph

Writing and recording this book has been a complete pleasure from start to finish. It's not every day you get to go into the studio with one of your musical heroes and ask them to demonstrate all of their licks.

As Martin has mentioned, this book was conceived as a phrase book for guitarists looking to learn the language of jazz soloing and when we set about gathering the material, it seemed the easiest thing to do was to ask Martin to use a pedal to loop some common jazz sequences, hit record on the camera, and let him play for 20 minutes.

The beauty of this approach was that we could see how Martin took a small seed of an idea and let it grow throughout the solo. When he felt that idea had blossomed, he took a few bars break and began with a different seed. It really hit home how the greatest jazz solos often build out of tiny, yet powerful pieces of vocabulary that combine to tell a story which gradually unfolds throughout the choruses – and Martin is certainly one of the greatest jazz storytellers in the world. He talks about his process in more detail in his previous book *Single Note Soloing for Jazz Guitar*.

We spent a day in the studio drinking coffee and recording, and in fact we gathered enough material for at least two more books. This book turned into the beginner-intermediate phrase book, and we will soon release its intermediate-advanced companion. Martin also recorded a whole load of longer solos and soon these will become a book of jazz guitar etudes. These will teach you how to organically develop a musical idea throughout a solo – another idea Martin covers in depth in *Single Note Soloing for Jazz Guitar*.

Once the recording was done, we cut the long videos into individual licks and sent them off to the annoyingly talented Levi Clay for transcription. He worked his magic and we could begin assembling the book.

Martin has requested that we tread very lightly on the theory when it comes to these phrases because he wants you to focus on sound, phrasing and developing the language – just as you did as a child. There's no need to over-think these ideas. If it helps to reassure you, most of Martin's playing is based on a diatonic foundation and tension is created by "filling the gaps" with chromatic passing notes, rather than by applying complex theoretical ideas.

We've organised this book into language that fits over different common sequences, so not only will you learn to recognise these progressions by ear when they occur in music, you'll have an idea of the type of vocabulary that works in that situation. However, there's a much broader point here that I want you to think about.

In language, the same words and sentences will work in an almost infinite number of contexts, and once you understand how the words work you can use them almost anywhere. You can make conversation with almost anyone who speaks your language, even if they're from a massively different background or location. The language of jazz soloing is no different. Once you understand the vocabulary you can adapt it to any new chord sequence.

Rarely do we get such direct insight into the language of a true jazz guitar master. Learn it, then go and make it your own.

Joseph

How to Use This book

When you open a traditional language phrase book, you'll see that the phrases are organised into "situations". The opening section might address greetings, the next might look at ordering food in a restaurant, which could be followed by directions to famous landmarks and so on…

This jazz soloing phrase book is organised into situations too, but our situations are the chord sequences you'll solo over in common jazz standards.

We've taken eight common chord sequences and taught you some essential vocabulary for each. However, just as with spoken language, the vocabulary you use to greet someone on the street can also be used in a restaurant or shop. In other words, phrases learnt for one musical situation are often appropriate in other contexts too.

After learning your first few sentences, you'll begin to pick up on the natural patterns, pronunciation and grammar of the language, so it gets quicker and quicker to learn new phrases and speak with authority.

In this book, you'll learn the perfect vocabulary for the following chord sequence "situations".

- Major to minor II V Is

- Minor ii V i

- I vi ii V turnarounds

- Dominant 7 chords moving in 5ths

- Static dominant 7 chords

- II V sequences descending in semitones

- Static minor 7th chords

- The minor blues

These chord sequences form the backbone of hundreds of jazz standards and by learning phrases for each one you'll quickly learn to "speak jazz" authentically. As these ideas naturally combine and get rooted into your subconscious, they'll quickly begin to influence the sound of the phrases you create yourself when improvising.

To use this book effectively, try to spot the chord sequences listed above when they occur in tunes you're working on. If you're working on a song with a lot of II V Is, you could begin in Chapter One. If you're working on a rhythm changes (I vi ii V) tune like *I Got Rhythm* or *Oleo*, you could begin with Chapter Three.

Next, *audition* the phrases in that chapter by listening to the audio examples. If there's one that really jumps out at you and you think it matches your current ability, that's the one you should learn first. It jumped out at you for a reason.

Just like our spoken language, we often reuse phrases that resonated with us when we first heard them. If you only *learn* phrases you like, you will only *play* phrases you like. Well, most of the time!

By being selective about which phrases you learn and repeat, you can control the musical language that you internalise, and which will become the source material for your own creativity.

When you sit down to learn a phrase, make a commitment to yourself to memorise it. To play anything fluently it needs to become a part of you.

To memorise a line, break it up into small rhythmic chunks of just a few beats and repeat each chunk until you can't get it wrong. When you come to Example 1a in Chapter One, for example, you'll see that it falls naturally into three distinct sections. Learn the first short section by listening to and copying Martin's playing, then play it over a backing track where it would occur in the lick, leaving silence during the rest of the phrase. When you can't get it wrong, move on to the next section and repeat the process. Next, combine the first two sections and play them until they're fluent before adding the third. Remember, you're not just learning a lick, you're programming yourself with how the language feels.

Once you've memorised a line, you should start using it in an actual solo as soon as possible. To begin with, try to play it perfectly at the appropriate point in the tune. After a while, your musical brain will start to want to vary the phrase. Don't fight this! These phrases are just a starting point for you. The idea is to teach you the language so you can form your own unique sentences.

As you gradually add more and more phrases to your vocabulary, they'll combine and evolve to create your own voice on the guitar.

Get the Audio

The audio files for this book are available to download for free from **www.fundamental-changes.com.** The link is in the top right-hand corner. Click on the "Guitar" link then simply select this book title from the drop-down menu and follow the instructions to get the audio.

We recommend that you download the files directly to your computer, not to your tablet, and extract them there before adding them to your media library. You can then put them onto your tablet, iPod or burn them to CD. On the download page there are instructions and we also provide technical support via the contact form.

For over 350 free guitar lessons with videos check out:

www.fundamental-changes.com

Over 11,000 fans on Facebook: **FundamentalChangesInGuitar**

Tag us for a share on Instagram: **FundamentalChanges**

Get the Video

As a special bonus to buyers of this book, Martin Taylor has released some videos of the more challenging licks, so you can see exactly how he plays them, and pause and rewind if necessary. These are not available anywhere else online. Follow this link to view/download the content:

https://www.fundamental-changes.com/martin-taylor-beginner-jazz-licks-videos/

Or use the short link:

https://bit.ly/2YJNg6C

If you type above link into a browser, please note that there is no "www."

You can also scan the QR code below to view the videos on your smartphone:

Chapter One – Major II V I to Minor II V I Licks

In most jazz guitar lick books, you'll find isolated Major ii V I ideas and isolated minor ii V i ideas. These can be useful (in the next chapter we'll look at plenty of minor ii V ideas) but I wanted to begin by teaching you phrases in a more musical context. When you learn licks in isolation, there is a tendency for your solos to become disjointed. You'll finish one idea. Then. Think about the next. Then play it. Before stopping… Just like the previous few sentences!

Jazz isn't like that. The lines flow like water across the chord changes. So, if you want to create a beautiful flow, you need to think beyond the phrase you're playing at that moment.

In this chapter you'll link together phrases that span a loop of the famous jazz standard *Autumn Leaves*. It begins with a Major ii V I (Am7 – D7 – GMaj7) and ends with a minor ii V i (F#m7b5 – B7 – Em). Normally, these are played over eight bars, but we've compressed them down to four. They'll all work as 1/8th note lines too though, so don't panic!

Because I'm *not* going to give you a breakdown of every single line, I want you to audition the phrases using the audio tracks and learn the ones you like. However, I did want to talk about the first few examples in this chapter because they're good examples of my approach and really teach you the structure of a great jazz line.

Take a look at Example 1a. Notice how the shape and rhythm of the first few notes is retained and developed throughout the line to keep the flow going across the chord changes. At no point does it feel like I'm playing unrelated licks over each chord.

In Example 1b, I develop the idea a little further to create a whole new phrase.

Example 1c is driven by a strong rhythm and melodic shape. It almost unfolds like a short poem.

Example 1d comes to a full stop on the GMaj7 chord, but a flow into the minor ii V is created by beginning the next "sentence" a few beats before the F#m7b5.

As you will hear throughout, leaving gaps in your "speech" is very important. Saxophone and trumpet players need to take a breath between playing streams of notes, so there are natural pauses and clearer phrases. Because guitarists don't need to take a breath, it's easy to overplay. It's important to remember to take "breaths" and you'll hear this clearly in Example 1e where the melody doesn't even begin until just before the GMaj7. These pauses are musical and interesting to your listener.

The end of the phrase finishes with a much longer contrasting phrase that drives through the final three chords. Learn the melodic shapes of this section and notice how I'm not too concerned about targeting chord tones here – it's the pattern and shape of the line that helps to drive it home.

The remaining phrases in the chapter continue in a similar vein. Notice how they flow and use strong rhythmic ideas to push onward through the changes. Almost everything is diatonic with chromatic notes added for colour.

The Major ii V I chord sequence is ubiquitous in jazz and occurs in hundreds of standards. Because it's a simple cadence, familiar to our ears, lines such as the ones that follow add shape and interest to phrases that would otherwise be arpeggio and scale based.

Understanding how Major ii V I lines sound and feel is at the core of developing a jazz language and you should learn these phrases carefully.

Begin by studying one line at a time and initially focus on just the first few notes. Play along with the audio until you can match the feel. Next, play these few notes over the backing track leaving space until the correct point in the progression comes around again. When you're confident, work on the next few notes and repeat the process until you can play the whole line fluently.

Also find backing tracks in new keys and play the vocabulary in different parts of the fretboard. The goal is to completely internalise one sentence before moving on to the next. When you have learned three or four phrases, something wonderful will happen: they'll begin to combine as you improvise over the backing track and will gradually evolve into your own unique language.

When you apply this language to new tunes you'll find that you'll immediately have something to say on any ii V sequences you come across. The bigger picture is that the understanding of the language you've developed here will help you to quickly play authentic-sounding jazz ideas on *any* section of the tune, almost by ear. The more vocabulary you learn, the more you'll have to say.

Here are some important standards you should know that contain Major ii V Is. There are hundreds, but this quick list should get you started. There will be a list of relevant tunes at the end of each section.

Important jazz standards that contain Major II V I chord sequences

- *All the Things You Are*

- *Autumn Leaves*

- *Here's That Rainy Day*

- *Line for Lyons*

- *The Nearness of You*

Before you start learning the following ideas, remember to audition them using the audio tracks and start with the one that jumps out at you. If you've not downloaded the audio already, you can get it from **www. fundamental-changes.com**.

Without further ado, here is a selection of Major ii V I jazz guitar phrases for your enjoyment.

Example 1a:

Example 1b:

Example 1c:

Example 1d:

Example 1e:

Example 1f:

Example 1g:

Example 1h:

Example 1i:

Example 1j:

Example 1k:

Example 1l:

Chapter Two – Minor ii V I Slow

The minor ii V is another extremely important sequence to master in jazz, and occurs almost as often as its Major ii V cousin. In the previous chapter you mastered many phrases that began on a Major ii V, and flowed through into the minor ii V. This means that the minor ii V phrase grew organically out of the Major ii V phrase and was strongly related to the original idea.

In this chapter I wanted to focus on the minor ii V exclusively and add some important new vocabulary to your phrase book.

Again, all the phrases are fairly diatonic and based around the appropriate scales and arpeggios but notice that I add chromaticism to create surprise and tension. The first note in bar two of Example 2a is the perfect example of this.

Audition these phrases by playing the audio examples first and begin by learning the one that most jumps out at you. Learn it by practicing in time with the audio, then play it by yourself against a backing track before moving on to the next one. When you have memorised it, move on to the next one. I suggest learning just two or three phrases before using a backing track to combine them with some of the ideas in the previous section.

When you're ready, try learning a new minor ii V tune from the list below, to apply your vocabulary in a musical setting.

Another productive practice idea is to copy a tiny part of the phrase which has a strong rhythm that you connect with. Try to keep playing that rhythm for as long as you can over the chord sequence. It's a powerful way to break out of the habit of playing regular 1/8th notes. Often guitarists assume that jazz soloing is just endless streams of 1/8th notes, but if you look at the notation below, you'll see it's anything but!

Important jazz standards that contain minor ii V i chord sequences

- *Alone Together*

- *Autumn Leaves*

- *Beautiful Love*

- *How Deep is the Ocean?*

- *Softly, as in a Morning Sunrise*

Example 2a:

Example 2b:

Example 2c:

Example 2d:

Example 2e:

Example 2f:

Example 2g:

Example 2h:

Example 2i:

Example 2j:

Example 2k

Example 2l

Example 2m

Example 2n

Example 2o

Example 2p:

Chapter Three – I vi ii V Slow and Fast

The I vi ii V chord sequence is the backbone of any "Rhythm Changes" tune, such as *I Got Rhythm* and *Oleo*. It is included here in its *diatonic* form (where all the chords naturally occur in the key) but you'll also see it played as variations, where all chords are dominant (I7 VI7 II7 V7), or with all the chords dominant except for the ii (I7 VI7 iim7 V7).

The following phrases are all played in the key of Bb Major (BbMaj7 – G7 – Cm7 – F7) as this is the most common key for rhythm changes, but it'd be useful for you to learn them in the key of G Major too.

The majority of the phrases in this chapter were played at a mid-tempo, which gives plenty of time to outline the chord changes, but the final five (3q-3t) were played a little more "up". Due to the number of chords, musicians will often use different types of vocabulary at different tempos and often simplify their playing as the speed increases. We don't quite get to that point in this book, but don't worry if you can't articulate all of these ideas at faster speeds.

Important jazz standards that contain I vi ii V chord sequences

- *I Got Rhythm*

- *Oleo*

- *Anthropology*

- *The Flintstones*

- *Moose the Mooche*

Example 3a:

Example 3b:

Example 3c:

Example 3d:

Example 3e:

Example 3f:

Example 3g:

Example 3h:

Example 3i:

Example 3j:

Example 3k:

Example 3l:

Example 3m:

Example 3n:

Example 3o:

Example 3p:

Fast Tempo Licks

Example 3q:

Example 3r:

Example 3s:

Example 3t:

Chapter Four – Dominant Cycle of Fifths

The bridge section of most rhythm changes tunes (see previous chapter) is formed from a cycle of dominant 7 chords that move in fifths.

In the key of Bb Major, this is most commonly played as D7 – G7 – C7 – F7.

I've included soloing phrases for this section for a few reasons. First of all, it nicely rounds off the previous chapter, as now you have vocabulary for the whole tune. Secondly, cycles of fifths pop up in a number of jazz standards which aren't rhythm changes, so it's an important movement to get used to – even if the chord qualities aren't always dominant 7. Also, this is a good opportunity to learn language that fits over a dominant chord that doesn't immediately resolve to a Maj7 or min7 in the next bar.

It's a fairly advanced concept, but these phrases can also be *imposed* over other chords to create some "outside" interest over static chord progressions. Again, this book is about learning to speak the language of jazz soloing. Once you are able to speak a little bit, you'll find that these words can be used in all sorts of different places.

Just like the previous chapter, I've focused on mid-tempo phrases to get you started but also included some more up-tempo ideas at the end, to show you how the vocabulary can begin to change as the tempo increases. It's not just a case of playing the same thing but faster – usually the soloist's approach will become more simplified too.

As always, try to figure out what it is that drives each phrase. Rhythmic and melodic shapes that develop throughout the line are much more important than focusing on hitting a specific target note.

Important jazz standards that contain cycles of fifths sequences with dominants chords

* *Dexterity*

* *I Got Rhythm*

* *Oleo*

* *Scrapple from the Apple*

* *Sweet Georgia Brown*

Example 4a:

Example 4b:

Example 4c:

Example 4d:

Example 4e:

Example 4g:

Example 4h:

Example 4i:

Example 4j:

Fast Tempo Licks

Example 4k:

Example 4l:

Example 4m:

Example 4n:

Example 4o:

Chapter Five – Static D7 Vamp

There's a real art to sounding jazzy when there aren't any sequences of chord changes to guide your improvisation. Many soloists get stuck when faced with sixteen bars of the same chord, so understanding how to make these passages interesting is a vital tool in the box of any jazz guitarist.

These dominant chords can last for whole tunes, or for just a few bars, as in a Jazz Blues. Either way, they're a great way to learn authentic jazz vocabulary without having to worry about following chord changes.

Important jazz standards that contain static dominant chords

• *Almost all Jazz Blues tunes*

• *Cantaloupe Island*

• *Caravan*

• *Mercy, Mercy, Mercy*

• *Watermelon Man*

Example 5a:

Example 5b:

Example 5c:

Example 5d:

Example 5e:

Example 5f:

Example 5g:

Example 5h:

Example 5i:

Chapter Six – II Vs Moving in Half-Steps

This sequence consists of two ii V chords that repeat a half step apart. For example, Dm7 – G7, followed by Ebm7 – Ab7. This sequence does occasionally appear in tunes (such as Coltrane's *Moment's Notice*) and is quite often imposed over a static chord vamp to add movement, but we're including it here for a different reason.

When soloing, you'll often come across chord sequences that are unexpected and move a little unusually. When this happens, it can be difficult to keep the natural flow of a line moving smoothly. This chapter is an exercise in tailoring vocabulary to fit the unexpected twists and turns a jazz standard might throw at you. If you can do it here, you can do it anywhere.

The challenge is to develop a vocabulary that flows smoothly over the chords despite them moving in such a non-diatonic way. As mentioned earlier, the secret is to build lines that are based around strong rhythm and phrasing. Often the rhythm will be the driving force in a melody and have a bigger impact than the actual pitches themselves.

There's plenty of Major ii V vocabulary to learn in this chapter, so as always, audition the phrases using the audio tracks and start with the ones that most appeal… but don't lose sight of the bigger picture, which is to learn how to carry your language smoothly into slightly unexpected situations. Imagine you're a TV detective walking into a laundrette and discovering it's a front for a drugs factory!

Example 6a:

Example 6b:

Example 6c:

Example 6d:

Example 6e:

Example 6f:

Example 6g:

Example 6h:

Example 6i:

Example 6j:

Chapter Seven – Static Dorian

We're back to more common ground here with a static Dorian sequence that is played over a Dm9 or Dm7 chord. You can safely ignore the G7, which is only there to give the progression a bit of movement.

There are many tunes that contain long static min7 chord sections that require you to play Dorian solos for an extended time (such as Miles Davis' *So What* and John Coltrane's *Impressions*). Without any changes to target, many guitarists will rely solely on bluesy pentatonic vocabulary. The blues is definitely a part of the picture here and you'll certainly hear its influence in the following ideas, but using Dorian really adds depth to your solo and an authentic jazz colour.

There's a real art to making solos on static chords sound jazzy, so it's worth getting all of this vocabulary under your belt.

Important jazz standards that contain static minor 7 chords

*   *Chameleon*

*   *Footprints*

*   *Impressions*

*   *Little Sunflower*

*   *So What*

Example 7a:

Example 7b:

Example 7c:

Example 7d:

Example 7e:

Example 7f:

Example 7g:

Example 7h:

Example 7i:

Chapter Eight – Minor Blues

The minor blues is an essential jazz sequence that's fun to play and often there are quite a few changes added to the basic chords. The one thing that they all have in common though, is a move to the iv chord in bar five. In the key of C minor, this is a change to F minor.

The phrases in this chapter teach you some wonderful bluesy vocabulary over the first four bars and show you how to deal with the chord change in bar five. Sometimes the eight-bar phrases are split into two shorter examples to help you memorise them more easily, so make sure you learn them in conjunction with each other.

Important minor jazz blues jazz standards

- *Equinox*

- *Blue Trane*

- *Mr PC*

- *Israel*

- *Stolen Moments*

Example 8a:

Example 8b:

Example 8c:

Example 8d:

Example 8e:

Example 8f:

Example 8g:

Example 8h:

Example 8i:

Example 8j:

Example 8k:

Melody and Variation

The phrases in this book are an excellent musical starting point that will help you develop your own unique language as a jazz guitarist, but you may be wondering where to go from here. How do you create your own solos from the melodies of jazz tunes?

It's not advanced theory that makes a fantastic player, it's developing a jazz language based around the melody of the tune. The secret is to replace the word "improvisation" with the word *variation*.

The melody is the strongest part of the tune. You don't leave a concert humming a chord progression! Almost all jazz standards were originally vocal songs, which is why they have such strong, memorable tunes. This means you can create a strong, meaningful solo by staying close to the melody and adding small variations. Even if the audience don't understand what's going on musically, they'll feel that your variations are related to the melody they've just heard. It will create a strong, tangible experience for them.

Soloing by varying the melody gives you an entire *structure* and *framework* for your solo to exist in. You'll never get "lost in the chord changes" and, most importantly, you won't have to magically create a whole new musical theme on the spot.

Very often improvisation is taught in a way that says, "You can play this scale over this chord…" but this is too far removed from what actually happens when jazz musicians start improvising. The more intuitive, melodic approach is to *vary the melody*.

Each short variation I play is what leads to the next one. Everything I play is led by my ears, but they have been trained by years of listening, copying, experimenting and playing – just like how you learned to speak.

The best way to learn this skill is to listen to great musicians playing and recycle their ideas (I always joke with my students that we're helping the planet by recycling!) These approaches are used all the time and now you know what you're listening for, it should be easier to pick them out. Even if you don't copy their idea perfectly, listening to how other musicians approach this will help you understand the melodic shapes and rhythmic possibilities you can use.

Variation can transform even the most pedestrian of melodies into a jazz solo that has momentum and tells a story. Forget about the chord changes and trust your ears. Concentrate on learning to develop your variations. The goal is to embellish the tune and build into a creative solo. Simply and gradually expand the complexity of the variations until you're playing an exciting solo. The secret is to use small variations that take the melody somewhere new. If you can do this, your audience with be right there with you. As you improve this skill, you will naturally become able to start your solos with more intricate variations and jazzier improvisations. Your only goal for now, however, is to see how many ways you can find to vary the melody.

Developing a melody depends on a few things. First of all, you can create whatever melody you like as long as it is strong and reaches the target note at the right time. Second, the more "connecting" vocabulary you have at your disposal, the more interesting your improvised lines become.

Vocabulary is learned through study and immersion in a culture – understanding how the language is constructed; its grammar and subtle nuances. You learn vocabulary through learning licks, as you've done throughout this book. You've learnt some of my jazz language by copying my playing, but as you begin to develop your own vocabulary (by using these ideas and taking them in other directions) you'll be able to use that language to speak in your own voice.

One of the dangers with the guitar is that our fingers take over when we play. We can quickly fall into playing pet licks that are part of our muscle memory and "programmed" into our body. The wonderful thing about jazz is that it is all about expressing the musical ideas we hear in our heads. Singing a line, then playing it on guitar usually results in much more melodic ideas. They are also well-formed phrases, because we need to breathe! This technique can make the biggest difference to your ability as a jazz soloist. Think of a melodic line, sing it, then play it on guitar. This is a great discipline to develop. Your lines will quickly take on a vocal quality that is missed by the majority of guitarists.

When you combine this skill with all the vocabulary you've been learning, the vocabulary will begin to influence the lines you "hear" and your jazz soloing skills will quickly compound. In fact, at this point you can really stop worrying about scales and theory, because the lines you hear, sing and play will always work!

Above all, have fun and keep developing your vocabulary.

Martin.

By the Same Author

Martin Taylor Beyond Chord Melody

- Master 7 steps to perfect jazz guitar chord melody

- Learn to create your own beautiful jazz guitar arrangements

- Discover Martin's secret approach to chord melody playing

Martin Taylor - Walking Bass for Jazz Guitar

- Learn walking baselines from the internationally acclaimed master of jazz guitar

- Discover how to effortlessly combine jazz chords and walking basslines

- Become the ultimate jazz rhythm guitar player and accompanist

Martin Taylor Single Note Soloing for Jazz Guitar

- Learn a time-honoured method for jazz improvisation that puts music before theory

- The Think, Sing, Play method that in time will lead you to be able to play any line you think of

- How to refine your jazz vocabulary and develop your phrasing

Martin Taylor's Complete Jazz Guitar Method Compilation

- Three best-selling jazz guitar books in one definitive edition:

- Beyond Chord Melody

- Walking Bass for Jazz Guitar

- Single Note Soloing for Jazz Guitar

With almost 300 pages and hundreds of musical examples, Martin Taylor takes you on a journey through his virtuoso approaches to chord melody guitar, combining basslines with chords, and how to really solo like a jazz guitar icon.

Made in United States
North Haven, CT
14 June 2024

53634458R00039